John Hamilton

A letter to Theobald M'Kenna, Esq.:

Occasioned by a publication entitled A Memoire on some questions

respecting the projected union

John Hamilton

A letter to Theobald M'Kenna, Esq.:
Occasioned by a publication entitled A Memoire on some questions respecting the projected union

ISBN/EAN: 9783337728359

Printed in Europe, USA, Canada, Australia, Japan

Cover: Foto ©ninafisch / pixelio.de

More available books at **www.hansebooks.com**

A

LETTER

TO

THEOBALD M'KENNA, ESQ.

OCCASIONED BY A

PUBLICATION,

ENTITLED

A MEMOIRE ON SOME QUESTIONS

RESPECTING THE PROJECTED

UNION.

BY JOHN HAMILTON, ESQ.

Divide & impera.

DUBLIN:

PRINTED BY JAMES MOORE, COLLEGE-GREEN.

1799.

A

L E T T E R

TO

THEOBALD M'KENNA, ESQ.

OCCASIONED BY HIS MEMOIRE, &c.

SIR,

Y OUR memoire on some questions respecting the projected Union between Great Britain and Ireland, &c. is, I believe, the third argument that has appeared to endeavour to reconcile this kingdom to the measure of a legislative Union, and is written in a stile and with a temper so very different from the two first, is so apparently calculated to seduce men by the temperate and rational allurements, you hold out to them of moderate national rank and certain domestic securi-

A 2   ty,

ty, that you evidently build your hopes of fuccefs on the acquiefcence of the moft uninfluenced and refpected part of the community.

You have attempted this with an exterior of candour, which bears fo ftrong a femblance of reality, that had I not felt that your foundation were fo evidently unfubftantial, I fhould have been led to doubt whether your talents have not undergone a temporary fufpenfion, whether the enormities of the crimes we have juft paffed through may not have made you the victim of timidity without your perceiving it. But a more clofe obfervation of your memoire convinces me that it may lead to a divifion of the public mind, fatal in the extreme, and though I do not accufe you of having loft your national feelings, I give you credit for the beft motives in your endeavours to feduce your countrymen from the operation of theirs.

But though the vicious cruelties of which we have juft beheld our countrymen guilty, are to you and to me equally fources of difguft and fhame,—yet fomething has taught us to feek different modes of recovering the national character.—You at once furrender the Irifh as not fufceptible of reform from within, and in the outfet propofe the radical cure of amputation, by removing for ever the great domeftic caufe of irritation *.

* Page 1.

By

By this I underſtand you to mean the parliament, to it you attribute all our ills, our diſſen-
ſions, and our calamities, and to infer that our
want of energy ariſes from our complexity of
conſtitution.

When you attribute all theſe evils to our parliament, you muſt either allude to ſome univerſal
principle of miſtaken legiſlative conduct, or ſome
diſtinct inſtance of error and unſteadineſs, connected with ſome particular political ſubjects, that
have of late been the object of agitation in this
kingdom.

That the former of theſe did not lead to the
late rebellion, to me appears ſatisfactorily from
the deſcription of perſons by whom it was pro-
-moted, but ſtill more ſo from that of thoſe by
whom it was put down.—Had a general odium
towards the legiſlators of this kingdom kindled
an oppoſition to its acts, you would not have had
ſo far to ſeek for its latent ſprings and ſources.—
You would ſoon have deſcried the abettors
among the better ranks of ſociety; and not have
been driven to an almoſt chemical proceſs,
before you could trace its movers and their
motives.

That the political ſubjects latterly agitated
here were not the cauſe of it, you fairly argue
and I readily admit. I accuſe no religion of
aſcendancy in rebellion. Though I trace the fury
and the ſavage barbarities of Wexford to religious animoſity,—yet I do not aſſert or think
that

that originally they were sworn in to a religious warfare,—but you will allow me to say that their paffions were inflamed, and their exertions prolonged by religious awe and perfecuting animofity, that fectarial antipathy led to inhuman barbarities, and sufficiently evinced to the rational mind that Ireland was not then so devoid of bigotted animofity as to render it a country, the police of which ought to be furrendered either to the affociation of the lower order of people, or the bare terror of the bayonet of the mercenary.

My mind fuggefts a very different fpecies of cure,—the calamities which you so juftly deplore, I attribute fundamentally to caufes exterior, and I neither confine them to the parliament nor to religious feuds,—they arofe in my mind from the intrigues of a power, aiming at the deftruction of Great Britain, and were facilitated by the erroneous governing principle infufed into our cabinet, by that power to which you are so folicitous, we fhould altogether furrender ourfelves. But I conceive it belongs to ourfelves, and to ourfelves alone, to create and eftablifh our means of fecurity.—Regeneration is a principle univerfally inherent, allowed to exift throughout all nature. Would you deny to your country alone the univerfal recuperative faculty? or would you voluntarily and gladly extinguifh it?

You

You fay * that Union in the abftract, does not ftrike you with that affemblage of horrors, &c. I will freely own, that in the abftract horror may be too ftrong an expreffion. But if it fhould prove unneceffary, unprofitable, and dangerous, 'tis enough without prefenting more hideous features. You talk of conditions in the abftract alfo—and again I admit, that in the nature of things two countries may be fo fituated as to allow of the confideration of conditions; but 'tis not fair to argue in the abftract, and found thereon a principle that fhould govern us. You muft fhew me that as we now ftand, in the exifting circumftances, it muft be moft eminently ferviceable, and the benefits not otherwife attainable, for unlefs you do fo, there is one fhort anfwer to all your pofitions. Independence is preferable to dependence—independence can procure us all we can defire, and therefore muft be retained.

You next proceed to argue, that our liberty may be as fecure under the fuperintendance of an imperial as a domeftic legiflature †. But here again your attachment to firft principles leads you into an error—for you forget the cardinal diftinction between the liberty of an individual, and the liberty of a ftate. You indeed, by your fubfequent definition of perfonal liberty, fhew that you build your reafoning thereon—your reafoning on this part of the fubject I fhall not

* Page 1.   † Page 2.

controvert,

controvert, but I contend, that it contains no argument whatſoever, applicable to the preſent caſe. I do not fear that the Union will ſubject us to an annihilation of Magna Charta, or an unneceſſary ſuſpenſion of the Habeas Corpus act. Theſe are rights that are common to all his Majeſty's ſubjects, and the Engliſh are intereſted in the ſupport of them equally with ourſelves. But there are many ſubjects on which an equality and reciprocity of privilege are not ſo unintereſting to England, the regulation of trade is a ſubject on which the people of Great Britain have been hitherto very ſolicitous to prevent our being placed on an equal footing, and the proportion we are to bear of public expenditure is becoming ſo, the rank we now hold in point of trade was obtained againſt their wiſhes, and has been retained with an eye of envy—of envy principally exiſting among the Engliſh mercantile intereſt, amongſt whom the miniſter muſt ever raiſe his loans, and to whom he muſt ever partially incline. Theſe are ſubjects, that without pretending to much penetration, I can diſcover many grounds to form a conjecture, that the rights of the Iriſh nation may not be as ſecure under an imperial legiſlature; and therefore I ſhudder at the ſurrender of our domeſtic one.

While America was ſubject to Great Britain, I never heard that any national infringement of the perſonal liberty of the colonial inhabitant was complained of—the Engliſh conſtitution was

extended

extended that fcarcely civilized people, but the national rights were not fo readily allowed by the imperial legiflature ; they thought the Colonies were fit fubjects for national depreffion, to promote the national elevation of the mother country, and by proceeding on that principle, they drove them to a rebellion, which ended in American independence. Before 1782, Great Britain, I may fay, legiflated for us, and before that time our perfonal liberty was well fecured, but our trade was not; there the rivalfhip ftepped in, and you may have feen that the bankers and merchants of Dublin have attributed our unprecedented progreffion in profperity, not to the impartial laws of the formerly rejected, but now in tended imperial legiflature, but to the wifdom of our newly obtained domeftic and felf-interefted parliament *.

When you talk † of erecting an independent government on every ten fquare miles of Europe, forgive my faying, you defcend below any title to notice. If there is one fo frantic Politician in this kingdom, to him let your reafoning apply ; but I conceive the finger of nature in general points out the line of demarcation. Though in continental fituations this may better admit of controverfy, yet even there a chain of mountain or large rapid river fatisfies all but inordinate ambition ; but furely our infular fituation might

* See Refolution of Merchants of Dublin.
† Page 3.

B   have

have protected us from the farcaftic line of argument you refort to. Had the moft eccentric of the French Directory, at the moment of the greateft elevation of the Republic, applied your reafoning to England, and founded on her comparatively fmall extent of territory a claim to imperial legiflation, even the enthufiafm of republicans would have fmiled; yet, believe me, I do not conceive the idea more extravagant than yours.

You next proceed to argue * that our imperial rank will receive an acceffion from the furrender; how you mean to prove this I confefs is a matter of fome myftery. I have heard indeed an argument held out to induce the borough proprietor to accede to the meafure, that one feat in the parliament which reprefented three kingdoms was equal in value to three in a parliament reprefenting one; how true that calculation may be, and what effect your pofition will have on them, I leave to their confideration; but, if you ferioufly mean to argue that Ireland infeparably connected with the crown of Great Britain, and poffeffed of an independent legiflature, will raife its eftimation in the eyes of Europe as a kingdom by becoming a province, with the power of contributing one-fixth to the reprefentation of Great Britain, I feel that you will have but few to fupport you. As well might a mighty lorded intereft attempt to perfuade an independent country gentleman, that

* Page 4.

by

by furrendering to him irrevocably the votes of an inferior intereft, the power of making leafes, the choice of tenants, nay, the modifications of family fettlements, he would increafe his profperity and refpectability, from being affured that his tenantry fhould always form a part of the lord's intereft at the election.

You next tell us †, that laws we do, and ever muft receive from Great Britain; but here again your general pofition furnifhes an argument of which you make ufe, but which when examined radically fails in its application. You forget that fituated as this country and Great Britain are, there muft exift an imperial general code of laws, as well as a national and local one. When you fay that we muft ever receive laws from Great Britain, had you added the word, *imperial*, every man muft have acquiefced; but when you fpeak generally, and include local appropriate regulations, every Irifhman fhould diffent. It is to me equally paradoxical that Ireland fhould *force* imperial laws on Great Britain, as that fhe fhould *compel* us to obey her moft probably unjuft regulating edicts relating to our domeftic arrangements, not obvioufly clafhing with general imperial advantage, though poffibly oppofite to her diftinct emolument. Here the rivalry of trade occurs, and here we require a legiflature of our own to defend our infancy, and check and expofe their power and intrigue. Here our local

† Page 4.

B 2

broils

broils may call, in our equally imperfect fystem of police, for laws that in a country fo matured may be received with difguft. I defy the information of a Britifh parliament to provide againft every exigency of the latter; and I much doubt whether they will ever fatisfy this kingdom that they are difinterefted in their decifion on the former.

Suppofe that previous to the firft appearance of our late unhappy rebellion, we had been reprefented in the Britifh Houfe of Commons by eighty Irifh members. We have feen with what ftruggles the bills for the fuppreffion of feditious meetings were carried through the legiflature in that country. Had the innovations on the received freedom of difcuffion in that kingdom, and the extenfion of the treafon law as confined to Great Britain, been accompanied with our fystem of infurrection laws as relating to us, had the minifter then introduced a bill for fubjecting to death in any part of the dominions regulated by the parliament he then addreffed, a man who took an oath to conceal a fecret however treafonable, for enforcing magiftrates to exact all the enormities of the execrable Corfew, and for tranfportation without a jury condemnation, how triumphantly would an Englifh oppofition have refifted fuch innovations! Not fmarting under the circumftances that juftified them, he could never have been convinced of their neceffity; he would have told the kingdom that their being enacted for the correction of our people was but introductory to

their

their inftitution as the fcourge of them; the Englifh might have recoiled at the profpect of fuch a fuperaddition to the innovations introduced among them; the minifter would have fubmitted to a diftant, in preference to an imminent evil; we fhould have been facrificed to the felfifh or the generous effufions of Englifhmen, and our rebellion have arrived at an irrefiftible maturity, before we had power to oppofe or inveftigate it.

Here is an inftance where our focial exiftence might have been loft, from the want of conviction coming home to the underftanding of the reprefentative; but the danger is ftill ftronger when the conviction comes *too home.* Suppofe, that previous to the peace, we all fo earneftly defire, the meafure of an Union fhould be completed. Suppofe, as we all earneftly defire, that peace fhould open new fources of Britifh fpeculation and of Britifh trade, that our prefent Mediterranean fuperiority fhould lead to connexion beyond the Straits of Gibraltar, that we have hitherto been unable to form; fhould the mercantile power of Great Britain ftrongly urge the exertions made for our prefent Premier during the variable conteft that now opens to fo glorious a termination; fhould fhe with energy reprefent the efforts made by Great Britain, and without exaggeration reprefent the obftruction offered by our rebellion, —do you think that every minifter would feel himfelf bound to exert his ufual influence to prevent national attachment to themfelves, and national averfion averſion from us, from operating as it might on the Engliſh parliament, in ſecuring ſome little trifling pre-eminence that might with their *capital* be every thing? Would the knowledge of our re. preſentatives avail againſt it? Or would this nation feel they were equally dealt with? I fear not —I may be miſtaken, but I am ſure I argue truly as to men and to nations, as far as hiſtory affords example; and I ſincerely hope my country may never make an experiment with example againſt them. I fervently pray ſhe may never ſuffer even England to legiſlate for her internally, nor ever offer to legiſlate for England imperially.

The feelings which have dictated the obſervations I have juſt concluded, afford a deciſive anſwer to the next paragraphs of the memoire, I ſay the next, for I paſs over the proofs of the utility of cultivating the Engliſh connexion with every reaſonable aſſiduity. Every man acknowledges the inſeparability of the connexion, and we agree in the common poſition, that it is only *how* it is to be moſt cemented that is now to be conſidered. It is advanced * that we are, if not legally, certainly effectively pledged to ſupport the credit of Great Britain. Every argument produced from this I admit to be unanſwerable, and I admit your poſition, with this addition, *in proportion to our means*: but, Sir, *that trifling addition*, to my comprehenſion involves the whole of the diſtinction between an imperial and an internal *national*

* Page 6.

legiſlature.

legiflature. I think we are the beſt judges of our
means, I truſt we ſhall never be illiberal, but we
are too much in our infancy to bear up againſt ex-
travagance. I can foreſee, in the complacency
and indolence of a Britiſh parliament, an abſolute
ſurrender of the queſtion of *Iriſh finance* to the
budget propoſal of the premier. I can foreſee
the difficulties and the danger of the premier to
lead to improvident and unnatural impoſition; but
I can foreſee no means of redreſs : an impeach-
ment would prove abortive, oppoſition rebellion ;
but I cannot foreſee that a domeſtic legiſlature with
a miniſter of our own would admit of a proportion much beyond our means. The Chancellor of
the Iriſh Exchequer would not pledge himſelf for
an Iriſh remittance he was not ſure he could raiſe.
He could not be ſure of one beyond proportion ; if he exacted beyond bounds he is reſpon-
ſible to ourſelves for the miſtake, and will be leſs
liable to be guilty of one. Let not then the op-
ponents of the Union be taxed with unwilling-
neſs to aſſiſt Great Britain, to contribute the ut-
moſt of their means to ſupport her naval glory ;
they only aſk to have a power of ſecuring and
amending the contributory ſyſtem, of judging of
its equality, and of apportioning its burthen.

You next * proceed to awaken our ardour to
the connexion between the two kingdoms. Were
you addreſſing the miſerable hordes of deluded
rebels, who have acted upon the principles of

* Page 7.

French

French attachment, your reaſoning might apply, but it has been my lot to participate military la-bour with you during the ſtruggle between the French and Iriſh parties in this country,— and I feel myſelf authorized to aſk you, do you think that the reſpected and momentous power of this country, even counting it numeri-cally, needs your ſtimulating rehearſal of Britiſh power, to rouſe and inſtigate their zeal for Britiſh connexion? I thought every man I could deem worthy of aſſociation acted upon the con-viction of it.—I remember the enthuſiaſtic ſtrug-gle that drove men, till then almoſt effeminate in their habits, to manly exertions, incredible and unexampled.—I ſaw the gouty honorary mem-bers of our yeomanry body, forget their inabili-ty and carry arms with thoſe by whom they had been excuſed, and with vigour and energy that ſeemed ſupernatural;—and I thought that French repulſion, and Britiſh connexion, were the ſecret ſprings of animation that wrought ſo powerfully and ſo ſucceſsfully. I ſaw the Britiſh auxiliary force arrive amidſt the plaudits of our city,—and every door opened with amplified Iriſh hoſpita-lity for their reception.—I ſaw in every man that true interchange of connexion, that the mutual danger and the mutual aſſiſtance led to—and I attributed it to that cauſe.—I ſaw it in you equal-ly with others,—but I did not attribute it to any partiality to the ſiſter nation *, nor to your wiſh

* Page 9.

to

to convince me that an Irish catholic is fufceptible * of the glory of the Britifh empire.—I
admit your memoire glows ftrongly with that
partiality,—And I doubt not its fincerity, while I
attempt to expofe the falfe conclufions it has fug-
gefted.

You talk next † of the popular queftions in
which you fay had the parliament been fo confti-
tuted, as to have followed the minority into the
popular notion of the day, there would have been
an end of, &c. &c. If you mean by this a panegy-
ric on the conftitution of our parliament, I am
in no manner bound to controvert you,—but I
would afk you, have parliament hitherto preferv-
ed the connexion ? With one folitary exception
there has not been an inftance of any thing leading to the reverfe—that exception was the re-
gency, an occurrence very explainable on almoft
conftitutional grounds, but which a condemned
omiffion of our fœderal connexion rendered poffible.—How many inftances have we had of co-
operation ? If you really fear feparative mea-
fures on imperial fubjects, I have already ceded
the point to Great Britain, but I own I do not
fee the pronenefs to feparation in our legiflative
bodies, that fhould deter the general minifter
from cordial co-operation with us, or that
any circuitous or complex ‡ mode of proceeding, oppofes our unanimity on queftions of im-

perial importance.—You talk of our independ-
ant government taking orders from a power we
do not recognize, and for remedy recommend us
to adopt that power as our fole governing medium, and thereby fecure permanent fettlement,
—thus you argue that the power which now
agitates us, through a domeftic legiflative, would,
through a foreign, cloath us in the comforts of
induftry. Can a power of fuch omnipotence be
fo unpropitious as to require a felfifh participation of our government, or refolve that otherwife we fhall remain deprived of the means of induftry ? If fhe does, fhe has fome finifter fcheme
to forward, and I deprecate the furrender to her
ambition.

You next * proceed to argue that from want
of capital, our commercial conceffions can at-
chieve nothing, and that nothing can induce
foreign capital but a change of manners, which
change of manners cannot be effected but by a
great change of conftitution. I fhall, when we
come to talk of police, endeavour to prove that
a Union would deftroy what little police we have,
and that thereby the introduction of foreign capital would be repelled. But let me here endeavour to controvert your pofitions by denying the
facts you build upon. If you fay that our profperity has not increafed fince the year 1782, you
are the only man in the kingdom that thinks fo.
If the increafe of civilization, extenfion of ma-

* Pages 12, 13, 14.

nufacture,

nufacture, the progrefs of the fine arts, were ever
rapid almoft to a miracle in any country, they have
been in this. It is within my own obfervation to
have traced the gradual remedy of our diforders,
viz. wealth and induftry, advancing with a rapidity fcarcely to be paralleled.—Afk the northern
merchant, Did the different manufacturing towns
of the counties of Armagh, Down, &c. fupply the
quarterly fairs with linen cloth, previous to the
year 1780, as abundantly as they now do their
weekly markets? How many confiderable market
towns have been eftablifhed through the province
of Ulfter fince that period, that are weekly ex-
hibitions of the moft animating induftry, and
produce weekly diffufions of wealth and comfort
to the peafantry, throughout almoft the whole of
that comfortable diftrict? Is it not fpreading
with a rapidity that more than fatisfies, that afto-
nifhes? I have been told, that it is fcarcely five
years fince the linen manufacture was hardly
known in the county of Cavan, and that at this
moment, almoft every cabin enjoys the fruits of
it. If you have formed your ideas from your
own obfervation, Did you confider the eaftern
part of Ulfter, a year before the breaking out of
the deplorable rebellion, inferior in the comfort
and induftry of its inhabitants, to the moft in-
duftrious parts of England? Agriculture, I admit,
has not arrived at fo much perfection, manufacture is not yet fo general, but the improvements in
the former muft come down from the Superior,

C 2   and

and there the abfentee is to blame ; the great extent of the latter muft wait for a population proportionate, and all the capital of England could not force us to get on beyond a certain pace, which though I do not argue that we have kept up to, yet I contend for it we were fufficiently rapid to fatisfy every moderate fpeculatift.

Your obfervations * on the deficiency of our prefent or improved commercial fyftem, through the want of a fuperior jurifdiction to decide upon the breaches of the agreement, are, in my mind, fceptical indeed ; but, fuppofing that it is impoffible for two countries, each poffeffing a legiflature of their own, to regulate their Trade upon the bafis of equality and found policy—let me deprecate this monftrous proof of your avowed partiality for Great Britain, when you recommend her Legiflature as the impartial jurifdiction to judge of her own poffible aggreffion, and of our poffible innovation.—It is the firft time I ever heard a political fpeculatift advance that the more powerful nation was the impartial judge for the inferior to look up to, to decide queftions relating to the rival trade of both.—Surely, the firft ingredient in every fatisfactory jurifdiction muft be impartiality ; either we are likely to be rivals or we are not ; if we are not, we need no fuperior jurifdiction to appeal to ; if we are, I deprecate the furrender of every thing to the more

* Page 15.

powerful

powerful country—her decifion, though juft, could not produce fatisfaction.

You next talk of Scotland—This fubject has been fo much and fo ably handled in many of the publications fince this queftion has been agitated, that I certainly fhall not infert what muft be an extract from them—I fhall only obferve curforily, that I do not fee that an Union would remove our religious broils, (of which hereafter) and that I do not wifh to fee the peace of this country ob-tained through half a century of rebellion. Indeed, I undertake to affert, and I hope to prove, that if every gentleman of property and of fenfe in this kingdom would exert his influence as he ought, that one-fifth of that time without any unnatural revolution, would be enough to do away all that was dangerous of religious animofity, and to raife this kingdom to real rank in the eyes of Europe.

I have heard, indeed, from refpectable autho-rity, but yet have been compelled to doubt, that fome of our Catholic brethren have been induced to accede to the meafure, merely as they avow, becaufe the Orangemen oppofe it.—When a mind becomes fo malignant as to be ready to fur-render eternal privileges to gratify temporary re-fentment, to rivet its own difability and humilia-tion, barely to caft fome degradation on an op-ponent whofe bounty had fcarcely ceafed to flow towards it—I deem its opinion to have loft all title to public refpect; but I cannot be eafily perfuad-
ed

ed that men poffeffed of fuch feelings are confiderable in point of number—I no more believe
that the whole Catholic Body is fo impregnated
with envy, than I do that as a religion they promoted the rebellion.—However, it is vain to dif-
guife that much of that fpirit has efcaped in your
arguments *.—You reafon on it, becaufe you
have heard of it; you are, I know, incapable of
poffeffing it, and I hope there is no man, who, on
reflection, would be actuated by it.

You will give me credit for my obfervations on
the Orange Lodges, when I affure you that I am
not an Orangeman, and that I fincerely hope no
exigency of times will ever require me to become
one.—But in faying fo, my objection goes much
more to the general evil tendency of political
clubs, containing religious exclufion, than to the
particular principles on which the Orange Societies are founded, as far as I can learn from their
declarations and their conduct.—The Orange
inftitution has as yet been of fhort duration, it
had its commencement in the North, at a time
when religious animofity and republican fpirit
united to render the Proteftant the victim of a
fhort-lived and unnatural coalition between the
Diffenter and the Catholic.—It was at firft an
union or principle of felf-defence, it afterwards
broke out into acts of retaliation, not to be de-
fended I admit; yet I do not fee why the entire
of the offence fhould be vifited on the Proteftant;

* Page 16.

I feel

I feel convinced that the political fociety called Defenders led the way, and that every degree of opprobrium vifitable on the Orangemen as the continuers of a club, is alfo attributable to the Defender as an original promoter of an oppofite one.—It was a confiderable time before the diftinction reached the metropolis. And when did it arrive at any alarming degree of confequence here ? at a moment when the moft deep-rooted fyftem of anarchy and cruelty had broken out into a rebellion that threatened immediate deftruction to the Conftitution as eftablifhed by King William, and was then raging with all the fury religious enthufiafin could infpire, to the certain deftruction of every Proteftant, for that was a fufficient crime, and to the avowed annihilation of every thing Orange in the land *.—Now, Sir, do not attribute to me any of the epithets you are fo lavifh of, when I fay that I do not confider the extenfion of that body at that time an unnatural event ; their firft principle, as well as I can learn, was the defence of royalty—fo far they were commendable and ufeful; to diffeminate that principle at that moment among Proteftants of every age, education, and degree, was a moft ufeful and commendable duty ; the next principle was Proteftant felf-defence—I afk you, was

* It is a fact, that in the County of Wexford, a debate took place between fome rebel captains, whether a houfe fhould be deftroyed or not, when a plunderer in his fearch difcovered a pair of Orange hand fcreens, whereupon it was forthwith ordered to be demolifhed.

there

there not a great deal of Proteſtant danger to
juſtify ſuch a principle of aſſociation? Nay, I aſk
you farther, had the rebellion extended much
farther and been conducted with the ſame religious
barbarity wherewith it was carried on in Wexford, muſt not every Proteſtant in the kingdom
have fallen into the Orange Society, and have ſe-
parated himſelf from the Catholic? By the mer-
ciful interpoſition of Providence, the rebellion
was checked, and I think much merit is attributable to thoſe who had temper and good ſenſe to
reſiſt the baneful ſyſtem of political aſſociations;
but I do not attribute to thoſe who did not all the
venom, or any part of the ſpirit of revenge you
ſo liberally beſtow on them.

You * ſay that the ſpirit of revenge lingered
after victory, and that they claim a dominion
over their fellow-ſubjects—You paſs over in
ſilence the ſpirit of revenge that raged amidſt the
Catholics during the conflict, and on what do you
ground your charge?—I ſhould have expected
from your candour when you charge a body
(among whom certainly ſome of the moſt reſpect-
able members of the community are enrolled)
with revenge and love of power, that you would
have adduced ſome examples to ſupport you;—
they have openly again and again diſavowed every
thing like religious perſecution; they have pub-
liſhed extracts from their regulations, tending to
ſatisfy the Catholic, that unleſs he is an enemy to
his country, they bear no enmity towards him.—

I know,

* Page 17.

I know, indeed, that many acts of atrocity have
been attributed to the Orange party spirit, but I
know alfo, that many of thefe have been explain-
ed to me as not involving at all the queftion.—
I do not feel any conviction that the Orange
Lodges may not celebrate King William's birth-
day as I do myfelf, as the anniverfary of an event
that eftablifhed civil and religious fociety on principles of wifdom, toleration, and liberty ; they
may drink King William as a John Wefley, but
they fay they do not—you have given us no proof
that they do—they have publifhed refolutions
breathing toleration—you have not fhewn any to
the contrary, or produced examples of perfecu-
tion.

I have been led fo far into an inveftigation of
the origin, principles, and conduct of the Orange-
men, not from any wifh to be underftood as ap-
proving of their principles, but from a defire to
convince the Catholic that they are not fo ob-
jectionable as you and many others reprefent
them, and to endeavour to eftablifh this pofition,
that the man who would concede to the projected
Union on the principles either of alarm from, or
enmity towards the Orangemen, is poffeffed either
of fhameful timidity, or of ten-fold the malig-
nity he would attribute to them—To dread their
power, is to mock the government under which
we live ; to concede our everlaftingly irreco-
verable independence from the dread of a power
controuled by the government, of about three
D   years

years duration, and which, from the nature of
its inftitution, muft diffolve with the circumftances that led to its formation, would be an act
of equal intemperance with that of your com-
mitting fuicide to relieve you from a temporary
and naturally healing wound.

But without pretending to much penetration, I
can readily difcover a very infidious fcheme at the
bottom of all this abufe thrown out againft a
particular body of the Proteftants. A pamphlet
which came from unqueftionable authority *
has endeavoured, ftrange and incredible as it may
appear, to kindle anew the feeds of difunion between the Proteftant and the Catholic. It has
talked to the Catholics of their numbers and
their difabilities, and with much addrefs endeavours to filence the Catholic oppofition, and to
deter the Proteftant from the repugnance it was
natural to expect he would exprefs, by informing
the parties that " Great Britain is not pledged
" upon any fpecific principle to fupport one *
" fect more than the other, nor debarred by any
" tie from affifting the Catholic." Much has
been made of this affertion, to endeavour to convince the Catholic that under an Union his claims
would be more likely to be attended to. You af-
fift the government in the effect they wifhed that
obfervation to make upon the Catholic, by feed-
ing their animofity againft the whole Proteftant
body, and explaining the improbability of their

* I mean the one generally attributed to Mr. Cooke.

attaining

attaining their object from them, by painting the bigotry of the Orange Lodges. But let not the Catholic be feduced by the writer of that pamphlet; let him take into his confideration the concluding fentence of the paragraph from which the words above quoted are an extract, viz. "but if Ireland was once united to Great Britain by a legiflative Union, and the maintenance of the Proteftant eftablifhment were made a fundamental article of that Union, then the whole power of the empire would be pledged to the church eftablifhment of Ireland."

But it may be whifpered, for it will not be more openly declared, that the maintenance of the Proteftant eftablifhment may not be made an article of the Union; that if the Proteftants oppofe it, and the Catholics confent, Great Britain is bound by no tie, not to fupport the Catholic in preference to the Proteftant. If you poffeffed the fame real love for the Irifh Catholic that your publication appears to breathe, you would have told them, as I do, that hopes founded on fuch principles will end in a fleeting and imaginary vifion. Let the Catholic look to the political hiftory of Great Britain during the period of the prefent minifter's power, and he will fee a fyftem of government that ought at one view to convince him of the fallacy of fuch expectations. Has he feen repeated efforts to repeal the teft acts rejected on folemn debate, and does he remember the principles whereon they were refufed? Does he know that ftate af-

cendancy

cendancy in its fulleſt extent was then as ſtrongly relied on, as at any period our hiſtory can afford? Does he remember the efforts of epiſcopal zeal to ſupport it, ſeconded and confirmed by almoſt the whole nation? And does he look to a reverſal of that entire ſyſtem, as the price of his acquieſcence to this degrading meaſure? The man who tells him ſo to hope is his worſt deceiver.—Let him look thro' the ſame period and trace the Iriſh hiſtory— What will he there find? a ſyſtem of conceſſion and conciliation—a change in his ſituation, extenſive and emancipating, every diſqualification ſeriouſly injurious, removed, none but a few diſabilities, rather of ambition than reality, remaining. This amelioration how obtained? from a Proteſtant parliament, moved, promoted, and ſecretly impelled by Proteſtant members, a vaſt number of moſt powerful families pledged to endeavour to have the ſyſtem continued, addreſſes procured and voted by Proteſtants declaratory of national fellow feeling and affection, men of honor and of talent their decided friends. Will he look to the parliament of a nation ſo diſpoſed and ſo proved as his mercileſs enemies, and aſſiſt in the annihilation of it out of pure envy, thereby ſealing the eternal continuation of thoſe diſqualifications that, as matters now ſtand, he has every reaſonable proſpect gradually to be relieved from? If he does, he becomes a victim to the intrigues of his enemies, and the folly of thoſe he eſteems his friends, and on ſo important a ſubject I can only

repeat

repeat the prayer of a celebrated Irish character now no more * : " that the God of Truth and of " Juſtice who has long favoured him, and has of " late looked down upon him with ſuch a peculiar " grace and glory of protection, may aſſiſt him " againſt the errors of thoſe that are honeſt, as " well as againſt the machinations of all that are f" not ſo."

I do not mean to accuſe you of being a dupe to ſuch ſchemes, much leſs to attribute to you any of the malevolence I think ſuch principles contain ; But, I merely ſtate that when you look to the Orange Lodges of this kingdom as a permanent obſtacle to the removal of the Catholic diſabilities, you attribute to them a ſyſtematic connexion, and a degree of weight, that they by no means appear to me to be entitled to. Why were they not in exiſtence to impede the conceſſions already made ? becauſe they were made before the rebellion had diſcovered religious fury, or before the perſonal aggreſſion on the northern Proteſtants. You tell the Catholic † " that the Orange men do " not feel their importance, that they overlook " that they ſupply almoſt entirely the labouring " and induſtrious claſſes in ſociety." I conceive the Orange men in their foundation to have ſpeculated upon a full conſideration of their importance rather than their impotence. I look to it as much more grounded in perſonal defence than political intrigue. I never heard of any Orange reſolution

* Mr. Flood.   † Page 19.

tending

tending to prevent further extenfion of privilege
to the Catholic body ; and I venture to prophefy
that fo foon as this country fhall be delivered
from the feeds and the impreffions of the rebellion
wherein we have been and are ftill engaged, when
perfonal infecurity fhall have ceafed to render focial intercourfe unattainable, when Irifhmen of
every defcription by mutual intercourfe fhall have
ceafed to dread each other, you will find our national feelings return to that ftate of harmony that you
and I may remember, and then in my compre-
henfion will the diftinction and the order of
Orange-men gradually and quickly be diffolved ;
and fhould the evils attendant upon fuch focieties
which you fo juftly detail, find any increafe in the
fpeed of their removal from your obfervations
thereon, I affert it will afford equal pleafure to
me as to you.

You are ingenuous in one part of your memoire. You fay you confider the Union more
eligible by the fyftem of police to which it leads,
than on any other confideration. I do not know
a better recommendation any meafure can carry
with it, than its leading to a good fyftem of police. But, it is on this ground that you and I
moft materially difagree, for I confider the hopes
of a compleat and general police as utterly deftroyed by the meafure ; and as I ground the abfence of Britifh capital principally on the want of
police, whereon you lay fo very powerful a ftrefs,

it

it is fair that I should with some anxiety endeavour
to establish my position.

If I understand the principle of a sound and
well regulated police, it consists of many parts,
and a co-operation of a number of gradations of
rank : it requires a resident gentleman independ-
ant in his property, dispassionate in his feeling,
influencing a surrounding yeomanry of respect-
able and comfortable establishment, who employ
with him the labourers of their district, to whom
he ensures justice and protection, and among
whom he enforces subordination, honesty and so-
briety by example, and, if necessary, by terror.
It is in the last stage that I look for the assistance
of the police man ; but you seem to look for him
in the first. My system appears to me to ensure
a circulation of property in the spot from whence
it is procured, an example of moderation, urba-
nity and justice, a set of men zealous to emu-
late it, and a still inferior set obeying it at first,
but gradually admiring, adopting and embracing
it. Your system appears to be from first to last a
system of terror, and a police regulated not by
principle but by the bayonet. We have been latterly forced perhaps to assist in compelling obedience
by force, but while I admit and deplore the ne-
cessity, I abjure the establishment of it as a permanent principle of government; and yet I confess
it is the only one an Union will suffer me to look
forward to.

When

When I fay fo, it is evident that I feel convinced that the fyftem of police I would recommend, would be for ever removed from our hopes
by the Union. Of my fyftem the refident Irifh
gentleman is the firft mover; of him I think the
Union would inevitably deprive us, there can be
no fyftem of internal police of which he muft not
of neceffity be the main fpring. It is not to the
rapacious agent, or to the temporary and grind-
ing middle tenant, I can look for either example
or popularity. They, as birds of paffage, look only
to the moment, and care not whether their objects are effected by the bayonet, or by voluntary
compact,—not fo the permanent holder, his intereft looks not only to the paffing fcene, but to
the fucceeding; every improvement in agriculture
and civilization, holds forth permanent im-
moveable amelioration, from him both muft flow,
and without him neither will increafe. We have
feen the effects of refidence and example, polifh-
ing and enlightening every corner of our ifle.
We have feen ourfelves horridly caft back to bar-
barifm. We behold the men of fortune, our beft
hope for reformation, balancing between a return
and an eternal feparation, and we are afked to caft
into the adverfe fcale, the eternal furrender of our
parliamentary rights, and with that the eternal
affurance of their feparation and indifference,
nay, their deteftation. Perhaps you may doubt
that the meafure of an Union would enfure the
removal of the Irifh gentleman. I confefs I do
not feel that much is neceffary to be faid on that

part

part of the fubject. Human nature, in my mind,
affords the beft argument. We have fcund that
an imperial court, and a numerous legiflature,
with the influence and anxiety attendant, have
proved very unequal to counter-balance even
fuch attractions, as the fo very fubordinate a
circle as our abfentees have moved in in Great
Britain has held out; the court and its append-
ages, may well be confidered as the *fun* of our
fyftem. Our fubordinate and inferior luminary,
even as it has been illuminated, has found it hard
to preferve a refpectable number of attendants.
It was found more profitable to be a fatellite attendant upon the firft mover, than a planet annexed to the fecondary, but when you deprive
us of all our cherifhing and attractive rays, I
fear our difk will become truly unilluminated
and opake.

And at what moment are our powers of attrac-
tion to be annihilated?—Is it when civilization
triumphed, when fubordination was acknowledg-
ed, when agriculture had been progreffively im-
proving, when a peaceful and happy refidence of
fix or feven fummers had attached the lord to his
foil; or when the eftablifhment of a number of
manufactories under his protection, and poffibly
with his pecuniary affiftance, had rendered his
continuance neceffary and delightful? Or is it
when he has fcarcely ventured to vifit his manfion, when every tree in his plantation has prefent-
ed a concealment for an affaffin, when his houfe

E

has

has been the receptacle of military defenders,
and his residence perhaps the country village
nearest his manfion, where alone he could fleep in
fafety? Muft it not be allowed that to perfuade
our men of property to live with us now, we
ought to be fuper-endowed with accumulated
means of conciliating their refidence, and not
be called upon to furrender all their confequence
and rivet their alienation?

How difficult we fhall find it, even fituated as
we are, to reconnect the orders of fociety in this
kingdom, is a melancholy reflection.—Our higher
ranks, from the various aggreffions they have
either fuftained perfonally or been witneffes to,
loathing and viewing with fear and abhorrence
thofe with whom they were accuftomed to interchange the neceffary duties of fociety,—while the
lower order of people, either from actual habit or
the frequency of public crimes, confidering as
trivial thofe offences, which, before they became
familiarized to, they hardly thought poffible, and
living in actual intercourfe with thofe who com-
mit them, whom formerly they would have
driven from their diftrict,—How tedious and la-
borious will it be to reunite them—and without
a reunion how is the country to become civilized
or endurable? Leave the Irifh peafant now to
his own meditations, and compel him to be de-
corous by bare dint of power, you will but con-
denfe and confirm, thofe principles of barbarity
and outrage, that as yet are but flightly imprint-
ed,

ed, but which on every opportunity will break
forth with reanimated force. But if by virtuous
example, and the efforts of interefted philan-
thropy, you caft a fhame upon their vices, the
native character may ftill throw off the newly introduced vices it is yet but acquiring; and the
reformation that is the refult of conviction, and
moral feeling, may become lafting and worthy of
our confidence. What a different profpect then
does our country prefent, when we contemplate the
abfence, and the refidence, of our men of property?

You labour much * to prove to us, that the
removal of the remaining catholic difqualifications is a matter of pure juftice, that it will have
the effect of reforming the national character,
but that it is incompatible with the exiftence of
Orange Lodges, and the prefent ftate of our
politics.—The difference between you and me on
this fubject, as to the effential point, is very immaterial. I abhor religious diftinctions as much
as you do. I hold the Catholic Loyalift in as high
eftimation as you do. I admire his ambition, I feel
for his vexation, when he fees others paffing to rank
in the ftate by means from whence he is excluded.
—But I do not hold the Orange Lodges as poffeffed of all the religious acrimony that you do;
—and if they were, I deny their ability to coun-
teract the Government, the Catholic, the Diffenter, and the Proteftants who are not Orangemen,
in their fchemes of extenfion of catholic privi-

* Pages 29, 30.

lege

lege whenever it can be judged expedient. You
say, the rebellion has furnished the Orange-men
with arguments againft the catholics, and you
fhew moft fatisfactorily that the rebellion fhould
not impede the progrefs of their caufe. I perfectly concur, and cail on you for equal candour,
to a pofition of mine, that though the rebellion
is not an argument againft the catholics fundamentally and permanently,—Yet it is a temporary bar to any great conftitutional change. It
has placed the country in a fituation that requires
the beft exertion of every man in the ftate, to be
directed to one object, the public peace. Catholic privilege is a queftion of awful importance,
the antecedent arrangements are numerous and
difficult. Their burdens are neither heavy or in-
tolerant, they ought hardly yet to have recovered from the joyous feelings, that recently removed reftrictions muft have created in them, and
though I am not one of their body, I venture to
affert in oppofition to you, that the mafs of the
Catholics are impreffed with feelings of affection
towards the mafs of the Proteftants, and I do
moft fincerely and difintereftedly recommend to
them to rely on fuch feelings, as the fureft
means of obtaining their grand object,—they
have the beft grounds for fuch reliance in the
patriotifm and liberality of this country at large
—in the certainty that fuch a meafure muft precede the true glory of this kingdom, and they
poffefs the beft and moft impreffive earneft, in the
concessions

conceffions already made.—Should they look to an Union for the means of it, certain muft be their difappointment. By the removal of the Parliament, the great object they now afpire to will be placed for ever beyond their reach.—It will prove, I affert, their trueft wifdom, to unite with the Proteftant to defend the Conftitution—They cannot fail, and at no diftant day, to become partakers of it.

This is a moment, I may fay, of mental ferment—'tis difficult to find any man capable of cool reflection.—Should the Catholic madly acquiefce in the propofed conftitutional furrender, in the hope of participating in the Englifh Legiflature, 1 have already endeavoured to prove that his hopes muft be fruitlefs—let us then look a little forward—Will this become a country for the refidence of Proteftants ? They are now poffeffed of a great proportion of the wealth of the country ; as fuch, with an additional increafe of Catholic confequence, obtained againft their will by an unconftitutional violation of the rights of every Irifhman, will many of them be likely to remain ? If not, the proportion of Catholics muft neceffarily increafe, and with that, their reftleffnefs under the prefent Church Eftablifhment, which you admit ought not to be altered*. When the public mind has recovered from its fever, the Catholic, increafed in his national proportion, rankling under the continuance of Church Afcendancy, admitted to no fhare in the

* Pages 29, 30.

miferable

miferable fhadow of reprefentation that will ab-
forb all the patronage of the Crown in this kingdom, will be apt to feel the addition of national
degradation to his own religious inferiority.—He
will lament that he affifted in the removal of that
Parliament, from whom he had received the means
of acquiring that wealth that has led to his ambition and his difappointment—He will feel difguft, that the means he looked to for the gratifica-
tion of his favourite objects, have proved the
eternal barrier to his attaining it—He will feel
with increafed difguft, that the whole was but a
fcheme for fubjecting his country to a foreign
tribute, fcarcely appearing to be voted by its reprefentatives.—The kingdom then, almoft wholly,
Catholic, will fpurn at the tributary connexion
with a nation wholly Proteftant; and then, indeed, will the Catholics, in a body, look to a feparation; then will every thing that has lately
paffed before our eyes, be reiterated with accumulated *vigour*, *but with palfied* oppofition, while
our unhappy country may fink beneath the ca-
lamity, fo low as hardly to be worth contending
for.

I ferioufly confider this meafure of an Union,
if carried, as the certain foundation of future attempts at feparation that will involve us in end-
lefs civil wars, and fubject us to inceffant attempts
by intrigues and falfe hopes to countenance
French connexion.—Look to the political hiftory of the world for the laft thirty years, and try

if

if the public mind has graduated towards flavery, or freedom—How individual was public exertion in America to fhake off the yoke of foreign power—How zealous was the fruitlefs and lamentable ftruggle of the Pole to preferve the connexion and independence of his country—How vaft is the power by which the conqueft is retained—How immenfely difproportionate were the numbers of the invading French army to the poffible exertions of the valiant Swifs—How honourable their oppofition even to a Republican Union,—How truly grievous their lot. But thefe exertions afford me abundant grounds for one affertion, that formed as the public mind now is, imperial conceffion is not at this moment a wife foundation for fœderal connexion.

You appear to me * as defirous of impreffing on the public mind, that whatever fhare of interference religion has had in the rebellion was attributable to the Catholic inferiority, which, as you hint, had vilified his mind.—This furnifhes me with one obfervation as to the propriety of agitating the public mind at this moment by the difcuffion of the Catholic queftion.—What are the difqualifications from which the Catholics have been relieved fince the year 1778, or I think I fhould rather afk, what is left that the Catholic peafant can complain of ? Have the various immunities to which he has been advanced, made

* Pages 26, 27.

n◦

no impreſſion on him ? Have they induced no gratitude, no pride, no ſelf-importance ? Has the effect of the conſtitutional prerogative that he has but once exerciſed already eſcaped from his mind, or does he think that he has poſſeſſed it from beyond the time of memory ? If he is ſo inſtructed, if he is taught that all he has obtained is immaterial, and can be perſuaded yet to be guilty of acts founded in bigotry and perſecution, he muſt be filled with a degree of ignorance, that never will admit the introduction of ſuch generous ſympathies as ought to precede final conſtitutional participation.

And the inſtance you adduce fortifies me— You ſay that when the Orange Societies made their appearance, the Catholics ſaw a myſterious aſſociation, and therefore ſought for arms—I ſay if they did ſo, they were ignorant and ungrateful—Had they looked to the Government for protection, they would have found it there— Had they looked to the Proteſtant for explanation, they would have found aſſurances that muſt have produced ſatisfaction, and in many inſtances, perhaps, co-operation ; but Catholics like thoſe of Wexford, who were induced to acts of unparallelled cruelty, by way of retaliation, forgot the Proteſtant Acts which had ſo recently benefited them—they yielded to the old inſtigation of religious vengeance, and as far as their numbers went, diſgraced their body ; ſuch men, you muſt admit, deſerve not imperial participation.——

When

When one partial act of myftery can counterbalance years of open and courted fraternity, the mind cannot be faid to be in a ftate fit for general affilia-tion.—If gradual conceffions do not as gradually do away antipathies that ought to be obfolete, no man can argue for equal participation.

I have faid that a moment of popular ferment is unfit for difcuffion of important ftate fubjects, and with that feeling I cannot help expreffing much difpleafure at the very inflammatory lan-guage* with which a writer of your profeffed mo-deration treats the remaining difqualifications of the Catholics in temporal matters, for the fpiritual you give up, and that too with an admiffion in the midft of them, " that it is idle, confidering " the number affected by them, to treat of them " at this day as a very oppreffive burthen." That opinion is in my mind too univerfal for you to combat, yet why do you accompany your admif-fion of it with declarations that " people meet " the affected fuperiority of a neighbour in daily " fupercilioufnefs of look and gefture, and in all " the ordinary offices of intercourfe," and with faying " that the affertion, that by the law of the " land I am your fuperior, is calculated to create " controverfy and pique ;" and you ! then accom-pany the proofs of the reftleffnefs of Proteftant fuperiority by the infertion of an Orange ftanza that could only influence minds as vulgar as that of the compofer of it. After the advances made

* Pages 29, 30, 31, 32.

towards

towards a good underſtanding between theſe reli-
gions you conceive ſo ſtrong in their rivalry, after the gradual progreſſion towards equality con-
ceded from the one to the other, with no oppreſ-
ſive burthen remaining, is it good ſenſe to recur
to ſuch ſtale and common-place obſervations, or
to inſert ſuch a paltry reviling? Is it that you fear
the Catholic body are too near an Union with
their Proteſtant fellow-ſubjects? I am ſure it is
not, for I believe you heartily wiſh to promote it;
but I muſt without ceremony ſay that I conſider
ſuch obſervations at this time to admit of moſt
dangerous conſequences. It is pretty well underſtood that the meaſure of an Union is not to be
forced againſt the wiſhes of the people, and it
is equally well underſtood that a great majority of
the Proteſtants are againſt it. If the government
are as deſirous of obtaining it as I believe them to
be, (truſting with perfect reliance on Mr. Pitt's
conviction of the importance of it to himſelf) I
know no means of furthering it ſo obvious as to
ſecure the acquieſcence, or even the indifference, of
the Catholic. And how can ſuch a ſcheme be
better promoted than by rekindling their animoſity towards the Proteſtant, by endeavours to
ſhew them that their intereſts are diſtinct, that it
will level at once ſuch ſupercilious ſuperiority,
and involve them both in one common degradation. Such arguments may for a moment create
a pauſe, but they contain too much fallacy to remain long with any operation; and I foreſee that
the

the detection of the infidious object held out will animate the oppofition to the meafure, and unite the whole kingdom in one univerfal burft of indignation and rejection.

After recounting a variety of caufes, which, as you conceive, led to the failure of the Catholic queftion, and which, whether they did or not, appear to me wholly inapplicable to the prefent fubject, you proceed * to fay, " that the train " of evils you have laid down are not within the " competence of the Irifh parliament to rectify." I really am at a lofs to difcover throughout your memoire what train of evils you allude to. You confine your obfervations generally to the Catholic queftion, on which you have dilated with confiderable force of argument, but I think it ill directed and ill timed. You endeavour to infufe into the Catholic the inadmiffibility of his claims through the medium of the Proteftant, and moft particularly defcribe the parliament as the place of all others where he muft make it with leaft hopes of fuccefs ; and the only manner your obfervations can apply to the queftion you propofe to treat of is, by your endeavours to reconcile to the Catholic the removal of a body hoftile to his advancement. A publication tending to raife fuch fentiments would have been wholly unexplainable, had you not avowed your partiality for Great Britain, and if the public mind had not required fome unnatural fubject to create a

* Page 38.

F 2   divifion,

divifion, for without fhewing the Catholic fome
extraneous ground to induce his concurrence, he
muft naturally be led to join the Proteftant in his
deteftation of the meafure.

I have already thrown out many grounds to induce the Catholic to confide in the Proteftant,
as the fure means of his attaining the removal of
fuch difqualifications as can be difpenfed with,
without the furrender of the fpiritual afcendancy.
How many men of experience, ability, and confequence in this kingdom ftand pledged to the
meafure at all times ? How many more have dif-
fented, not from general principles, but from
temporary motives, who have argued in concurrence with the received opinion of many able
ftatefmen, that great political changes fhould proceed gradually : that to level at once all religious
diftinctions in a ftate, would be to make an experiment, the iffue whereof might be fatal ? Has
the amount of the conceffions already made been
confiderable, and the progrefs of them rapid ?
Will not the religious diffenfion, while it exifts,
be an inconceivable drawback on the profperity
of the country ? Will it admit of our ever ven-
turing to engage in any national object that may
require univerfal coincidence of will and of action ? Will not intercourfe and focial communi-
cation break down the prejudices which ftand in
the way, and will not the general advantage to
the country prefs the matter forward, and carry
it into effect, in fpite of prejudice or party ? How

numerous

numerous and irrefiftible are the grounds whereon the Catholic fhould ftand with certainty for the full attainment of his wifhes, as matters now are? But how equally irrefiftible will be the obftacles he will have to encounter after the propofed change? You tell him that there are " extrava-" gant accumulations of fovereign powers in the " hands of a few men," which muft ftand for ever in their way. If there are fuch accumulations, let the Catholic examine the principles of thofe in whofe hands they are placed, and let him learn that many of them ftand pledged to the attainment of his object. Let him with difpaffionate reflection view his intereft as it ftands in the nation' and he will fee that his political fituation muft acquire gradual increafe; but how will it be loft in the fcale of the empire, when he parts with that parliament, of which alone he can ever be a partaker, and of which his body now conftitute a majority of the electors. Let him difcredit every fpeculatift who tells him that parliament are incompetent to his admiffion.

If you intended any allufion to the rebellion and the caufes of it, which you would argue that our parliament are incompetent to remove, I muft beg to exprefs my moft unqualified diffent. I think this is one of the moft prominent features where the fuperiority of a domeftic to a foreign parliament is difcoverable. Look to the code of laws calculated to meet every ftep in the gradation of rebellion, and which though unable to control

trol the unbounded exertions of our fecret enemies, yet were of the utmoft advantage in check-
ing and oppofing it. Look to the report of the
Committees of both Houfes. See the evidence
they waded through, written and unwritten:
could the developement of a myftery of fuch
complication have taken place in any other country, or by the inveftigation of any other parliament? Surely matters of this nature require the
prompt decifion and the accurate information of
a legiflative body acting on the very fpot where
the evil exifts.

I fhould have expected that a writer who feems
to have the fuccefs of the meafure fo much at
heart as you do, would not have confined
his arguments in fupport of it to a fhort ca-
talogue of evils to be removed, and totally omit
any perfuafive obfervations, grounded on advantages to be conferred.—Perhaps you tried it, and
having found, after deep refearch, that every attempt at argument, grounded on advantages to
be conferred, ended in a circle, you very pru-
dently relinquifhed that very operative mode of
conviction; and it would, in my mind, be equally
prudent in every writer on that fide of the queftion to follow your example.—Indeed, the moft
warm advocates for the meafure, confine their
promifes on that fide of the fubject to two points,
extremely defirable I confefs, viz. internal peace,
and external commerce; but I own I have heard
little

little to feduce me to confider either of them as likely to be improved by it.

As to the promotion of internal peace from the meafure, I have already mentioned the fubject, and endeavoured to argue that it would be much more injured than improved by it.—As to commerce, I certainly am unequal to go into the detail of the fubject, but there are a few thoughts that have occurred to me, as to the general probability of our being benefited by the change, that I fhall here fubjoin.

The great and leading objection to the furren der, in a commercial point of view, arifes from the degree of rivalfhip that already exifts between the two kingdoms on that fubject, and that is likely to encreafe as we get forward in profperity.—The oppofition of the Britifh merchants to the propofitions of 1785, which were of fo inconfiderable confequence as to be rejected by this kingdom, is one example worth a thoufand, to fatisfy us of their attachments to their own intereft.—Indeed, the general character of the Britifh merchant, the firft for enterprize and knowledge in every branch of trade with every corner of the globe, is known to be as univerfally eftablifhed for intrigue and exclufion;—add to this, the immenfe difference between us in point of capital—Will you attempt then to argue, that it is fafe to furrender our ftill infant manufacture, and far from matured trade, to the actual control of men elected and influenced by the Eng-

lifh

lifh merchant.—Though in every branch of legiflation the conceffion might be defirable, the
danger attendant upon this would, in my mind,
be a very fufficient counterbalance—this is the
great fource of our profperity—it is by this that
we are to attain to that rank, and that wealth,
that nature feems to have pointed out as our por-
tion, from our fituation and our internal refources;
and it ought not to be hazarded for any tranfitory
gratifications, fuppofing them even to exift.

But how is the great increafe of trade to be
promoted—Is it argued that Ireland is fituated
upon the map fo advantageoufly, as that fhe might
become a kind of emporium for the entire of
Europe to refort to for the purchafe of Weft
Indian commodities ?—In my apprehenfion not—
fhe contains admirable materials for fuccefs in the
promotion of manufactures of various kinds,
and will certainly arrive at population to make
ufe of every advantage fhe poffeffes ; but to talk
of foreign imports, all I would afk for her would
be, that fhe might arrive at the exclufive carrying and importing all the materials neceffary for
her confumption, and for her manufacture.——
England now, with little exception, enjoys the
carrying trade for both kingdoms—through her
we obtain moft of our fugars and Weft Indian
articles.—I fhould hope, indeed, that we might
foon obtain that by ourfelves ; but I have not
the vanity to afpire to be the carrier of Weft
India product for England, or the channel through
which

which fhe will receive it.—Let every man, therefore, who talks of encreafe of commerce, *be affured that* the diminution of confumption may not
counterbalance any advantage the meafure holds
out ; and the diminution, I fhould fear, would be
immenfe, when I confider that every abfentee
who leaves this kingdom draws with him at leaft
one artizan, and every artizan, perhaps, fix
working mechanics.—How this will operate a
few years will evince, with, I dread, moft melancholy proof.

My laft obfervation is grounded on a fuppofi-
tion, that our commercial fyftem is capable of
being amended by conceffions from Great Britain—Whether it be or not, is for thofe who are
verfed in the fubject to decide—from every thing
I have been able to learn on the fubject, our
commercial rank needs not, indeed is not fufceptible of, much improvement ; but admitting that
it does require fome alteration, and that Great
Britain is willing to purchafe our legiflative furrender by a grant of commercial immunity ; it
does not, in my mind, follow that we would be
prudent in accepting of the terms.—The benefit
derived to our trade may perhaps be counterba-
lanced by the injury fuftained by our private fecurity; the want of the latter may annihilate the
means of taking advantage of the former ; but,
above all, let every Irifhman confider—Has not
nature entitled us to as free a trade as Great
Britain.—You are eloquent and forcible in your

G   reafoning

reafoning upon the equality of the Irifh Catholic
and Proteftant, and triumphantly fay, " this
" world was made for Cæfar *," but your admitted partiality for Great Britain has blinded
your difcrimination as to the equality of the
Englifh and Irifh character, for you feem to me
to confider the equality of mankind, and the
equality of nations, as fubject to very different
modifications. For my part, 1 think better
of Great Britain, than you with all your predi-
lection appear to me to do, for I look forward
with hope, to the removal of every jealous re-
ftriction, if any exift—in the certainty that our
increafed connexion will lead to increafed affection,—but fhould it not, I ftill am againft " bar-
" tering conftitution for commerce," feeling
perfectly contented with the gradual advance
we have latterly made in trade and profperity,
and which ever increafes in its rapidity during its
progrefs.

It is faid and appears to be relied on, that parts
of this kingdom are likely to be much benefited in
a commercial point of view by the projected
Union,—and the the manly oppofition made by
Dublin, is fought to be frittered away by infinua-
tions, that the interefted feelings of its inhabitants, on account of the probable injury the metropolis would fuftain, was the true caufe of it.
This argument admits of one objection that tells

very

very ſtrongly againſt the meaſure to every part of the kingdom, viz. the injury to the metropolis.—Our rank amongſt nations in point of civiliſation is ſtill below mediocrity, our manners admit of ſtill conſiderable improvements, and the fine arts, I may ſay but lately introduced, have a vaſt journey indeed to travel, before they will arrive at an honourable maturity. It is by a metropolis of conſiderable extent, that the continuance of their progreſs among us can be ſecured. Will a deſerted and tumbling city induce amongſt us reſident artificers of eminence, or teachers of experience,—Will the ſtage, that great improver of taſte, and corrector of morals, already-ſo much on the decline, ever rear its head in a city deprived of its court and its wealth ?—Let not then a ſelfiſh hope of advancement hazard the proſpect of refinement among us, but let every man feel impreſſed with the opinion of a profound philoſopher *,—" that the ages of refinement are both " the happieſt and moſt virtuous "

There is another obſervation I would addreſs to the merchants of the ſouth, to whom I muſt be already underſtood to have alluded—which is, that a change of the direction of public trade can be no argument for the meaſure. If one part of the country is injured as much as the other is improved, there is little national feeling annexed to the man, who would for partial im-

* Mr. Hume.

provement

provement, furrender general independence.—
Befides, let the idea I have hinted on the fubject
of confumption be taken into confideration, and
let the fouthern merchant calculate whether even
fuppofing that the deftruction of the trade of
the metropolis would enfure the whole of it to
center there, the advantages might not be coun-
balanced by the general decreafe of confumption,
and whether he would not on the whole find his
fituation at leaft not bettered by the meafure.

There is a temporary argument againft the
meafure, which ftrikes me with a degree of force
that would render it criminal to pafs it over.—
I have ftated that in my apprehenfion, the firft
moment of cool deliberation after the meafure is
carried, would prefent this province to Great
Britain, compofed of difcontented Proteftants,
difappointed and betrayed Catholics, and de-
graded Diffenters.—The emiffaries of the French
republic found in this kingdom, notwith-
ftanding the loyalty it fhewed, a melancholy
number of our people whofe difcontents made
them fit objects for their fchemes. What increafe
this meafure might produce, I tremble to reflect
on. If this country, with the zealous ardour of
the yeomanry, and the love for the conftitution
they evinced, afforded to France fuch means of
attacking the power of Great Britain, as with a
view to it alone, to induce her to break off the
negotiations at Lifle; with what accumulated
force of argument will Mr. Tone's fucceffor at
a future

a future conference, recommend a repetition of the experiment among a nation, almoft to a man difcontented, and having 'no conftitution to infpire the inhabitants with a renewal of their ardour? I fay, France muft be frantic, not to yield to fuch argument; and that the meafure will lead irrefiftibly to a repetition of invafion, and the prolongation of a war, that has fo feverely fallen on every defcription of Britifh fubjects, though attended with unufual traits of glory.

Your concluding argument *, appears to me to afford but little ground, to diminifh the natural averfion we muft conceive to the adoption of the meafure.—You talk of the urgent intereft of the Imperial Government, of the neceffity of her bringing forward all the energies of its remaining territory; and when you talk of the neceffity of univerfal action againft France,— You tell us, that " her power muft fo terrify " the Britifh minifter, as to fhield us from in " juftice and partiality."—If nothing but an in terefted motive can enfure us a kind policy, it is not prudent to concede every thing to a tribunal fo felf-devoted. Every hour will not equally prefs her, and enforce her to be juft—in the moments of continental quiet, fhe might commercially annihilate us; and I like not the omnipotent power, that requires neceffity as the governing principle to lead to its juftice; attached,

* Page 41.

connected.

connected, and devoted, as we are, to one common fate,—muſt we ſurrender our intereſt to inſure our protection? Is our national importance ſo trivial, that without an Union the policy of England would be juſtified in being unkind,— I ſhould hope ſhe felt differently. Indeed, we have examples that ſhe does. The dependance of our parliament was long a bone of contention between the two kingdoms, the removal of the cauſe ſilenced the diſpute,—How many ſupporters had Great Britain during the rebellion of 1798,—that had the conſtitution remained as it was in 1781, would have been at beſt paſſive? It is not good policy to create anew a ſtumbling block, that has already been the ſubject of ſo much political antipathy. We now truly participate the Britiſh conſtitution, and would hazard every thing in its defence. But if you remove the ſource of our exertion, the effect of it may become in operative, by poſſibility repugnant.

The reaſons that 1 have offered, make me with much deciſion reject the diſcuſſion of the ſubject of an Union. It is a ſubject that appears to me to be fraught with internal danger, and external injury, and to call for an awful revolutionary ſurrrender, without any equivalent, or in any point of view, a ſubſtantial conſideration. Diſcuſſing it as a native of this country, it muſt be conſidered I feel a national prejudice, that may ſubject my opinion to the objection of intereſted conſideration,—Yet, I have endeavour-

ed

ed to divest myself of false and senseless pride, to view the subject in every shape of projected benefit ; and I have found it impossible to trace one solid advantage, that can arise to the kingdom from the measure. The disadvantages and dangers to which it subjects it, to my comprehension are manifold, and therefore, I feel myself sheltered from the charge of endeavouring to rouse in my countrymen a false pride, when I addrefs them by the general term of Irishmen, and call upon them as one people, that hope to coalesce and to form a powerful nation, the pride and sinew of Great Britain,—to speak forth regardless of distinction one voice, and to tell the empire with one unanimous declaration, that they feel, respect, and will maintain their freedom.

If this appeared to me to be the language of separation, I would be the last man in the state that could give it utterance ; but most fervently do I declare, that in no one point of view do I consider the Union more deplorable than in its tendency to a separation. One question it would seem might afford a proof of this, Has the connexion since 1782 been loosened or cemented? If my countrymen will attend to the language of that day, how forcibly does it apply to my opinion. Let it be remembered, that when the conceffion of Irish independence was avowed from the throne, the first emanation of Irish gratitude, and which was received with delight by the em-

pire

pire was, that " gratified as we were, we did
" affure his Majefty that no conflitutional quef-
" tion between the two nations would any longer
" exift, that could interrupt their harmony ; and
" that Great Britain, as fhe had approved of our
" firmnefs, fo might fhe rely on our affec-
" tion *."

Here was a parliamentary declaration voted by
many of our prefent reprefentatives, that the removal of conflitutional difqualifications muft
lead to national cement and co-operation. Surely
the recorded tranquil opinion of fuch men, at a
moment of national triumph, muft weigh more
in the opinion of Irifhmen, than the heated, if
not timid conception the prefent moment might
lead to. But we are not left to the bare decifion
of Irifh feeling on the fubject, for we have a recorded declaration of the Britifh Cabinet, pro-
nounced by a nobleman, whofe abilities now
contribute to the government of the united empire, that muft filence clamour, and render doubt
fhamelefs. We were addreffed through our legiflative bodies, at the conclufion of that memor-
able feffion, by his Grace the Duke of Portland,
in the following words : " The great and confti-
" tutional advantages you have fecured to your
" country, and the wife and magnanimous con-
" duct of Great Britain, in contributing to the
" fuccefs of your fteady and temperate exertions,
" call for my congratulations on the clofe of a

* Addrefs to the King, voted Monday, May 27, 1782.

" feffion,

" feſſion, which muſt ever reflect the higheſt ho-
" nour on the national character of both king-
" doms."

" It muſt be a moſt pleaſing conſideration to
" you to recollect, that in the advances you
" made towards the ſettlement of your conſtitu-
" tion, no acts of violence or impatience have
" marked their progreſs. A religious adherence
" to the laws confined your endeavours within
" the ſtricteſt bounds of loyalty and good order.
" Your claims were directed by the ſame ſpirit
" that gave riſe and ſtability to the liberty of
" Great Britain, and could not fail of ſucceſs,
" *as ſoon as the councils of that kingdom were in-*
" *fluenced by the avowed friends of the conſtitu-*
" *tion.*"

" Such a ſpirit of conſtitutional liberty com-
" municating itſelf from one kingdom to the
" other, muſt naturally produce that reciprocal
" confidence and mutual affection, of which we
" already begin to feel the moſt ſalutary effects.
" A grateful zeal and generous ardour have
" united this whole kingdom in the moſt cordial
" and vigorous exertions, which promiſe effect-
" ually to fruſtrate the deſigns of our common
" enemy, and to re-eſtabliſh and ſecure the glory
" of the whole empire*."

* Speech from the Throne, Saturday, July 27, 1782.

Here

Here is the language of an English senator,
the congratulatory addrefs to both kingdoms, on
Irifh emancipation. He has firft told *us* that the
advantages we then gained called for congratula-
tion; that the conduct of Great Britain in ceding
to our exertions was wife and magnanimous,
and that the *feffion muft for ever reflect the higheft*
honor on both kingdoms. May no fubfequent one
by the annihilation of the immunities we then
obtained, reflect the reverfe!!

He next commends our temperate conduct
during the ftruggle, and tells us, that we were
actuated by the fame fpirit that give rife and fta-
bility to the liberty of Great Britain; that *when*
the Britifh councils were influenced by the avowed
friends of the conftitution; that the caufe of Irifh
liberty could not fail of fucccfs; thus afferting that
Irifh liberty then formed a principle of the Britifh
conftitution.

He then affures you, *that the fpirit of confti-*
tutional liberty communicating itfelf from one king-
dom to the other, muft produce confidence and
affection.——How baneful may the ftuggle
againft flavery prove?—How injurious its example?—Could his Grace have forefeen the prefent
moment, and have wifhed to furnifh this country with an opinion againft the meafure, he could
fcarcely have conveyed more interefting truths
than thefe few ftrong fentences contain.

He lastly tells you that the con-
stitutional concession united the king-

DOM, AND ESTABLISHED THE GLORY OF THE
EMPIRE.

Should it prove the hard fate of our prefent
Chief Governor, to addrefs us on the 27th of
May 1799, when he may unfortunately be compelled to exercife his official duty in the Houfe of
Peers, by giving the Royal Affent to the Bill of
Union, if he wifhes to rank as a prophet, he
will accompany our fubjugation with a fpeech the
critical reverfe of that delivered at our glorious
emancipation.

But I fhould truft that event is not to be dreaded
—furely " our temperate and fteady exertions"
will have as much avail at all times in *retain-
ing* a Conftitution we poffefs, as they
had at that time in obtaining the conceffion of
one we did not. But that fuch exertions would
now be fuccefsful, admits of no doubt. It is
our peculiar good fortune that the Britifh Councils muft now be influenced by the fame fpirit;
that the wife Senator who gave us here that folemn admonition, to revere our Conftitution,
then newly acquired, is now the Secretary of
State for the Home Department in Great Britain,
and will unqueftionably prove the truth of the
adage, that

Cælum non animum mutant qui trans mare currunt.

May our patriotifm, good fenfe, and loyalty,
give Great Britain on this occafion, a fecond opportunity

portunity of commending " our fteady and " temperate firmnefs" in fupport of our rights, and may every fubfequent tranfaɛlion worthy being recorded in hiftory be a prominent proof of " our affeɛtion."

F I N I S.

THE Gentleman to whom this Letter is addressed, is requested to consider it as proceeding solely from the writer's wish to prevent *religious divisions* from operating so as to induce any class of his countrymen to be actuated at this moment by *prejudice*, to which, in his conception, the Memoire on the projected Union very forcibly leads.

He will also, should he deem it worthy of perusal, and light upon any expression that conveys to him a symptom of improper warmth, rest assured that it is directed to his arguments *only*, and accept the writer's apology.

www.ingramcontent.com/pod-product-compliance
Lightning Source LLC
Chambersburg PA
CBHW021631270326
41931CB00008B/965